RUMOURS OF LIGHT

Poems

by
Gideon Heugh

Copyright © 2021 by Gideon Heugh

All rights reserved

ISBN: 9798649272759

Cover design: Katie Tang

For my shining daughter

LIST OF POEMS

Prelude · It is time

IT IS TIME 3

I · Blackbird

NIGHT WILL FALL ON YOU 7
GENESIS 8
BLACKBIRD 10
SUNRISE 11
I JUST HAD THE MOST
UNPRODUCTIVE MORNING 12
CAMPING IN SPRING 13
WHEN GOD COMES TO VISIT 14
WAKING EARLY 16
THE GEESE 17
MIRACLES 18
STEPPING OUTSIDE AT FIRST LIGHT 20
HOW UNEXPECTED 21

THE LATE SPRING DAWN 22
A NEW LIGHT ARRIVES 23
HIDE AND SEEK.. 24
TO BEGIN THE DAY BRIGHT.................... 25
MOON SONG... 27
HOLD ON.. 28

II · *The cup you have*

I SEE YOU... 31
WHAT MANNER OF SACRED BEING 32
DOUBTS 33
HOW TO BE MORE ALIVE 34
LOVE 36
DON'T SETTLE 37
YOUR LIFE 38
MIRROR.. 40
WE TOO ARE SHINING BORN 41
THE CUP YOU HAVE 42
THERE YOU ARE 44
LET ME NOT BE GRACEFUL 45
SCALPEL... 46

AN ANCIENT TUNE 48
YOUR UNGODLY SOCKS 49
TO LIVE 50

III · Dark matter

CAGE 57
THE ELOQUENCE OF LIGHT 58
DARK MATTER 59
LONELINESS 60
THE DEATH OF GOD 61
BLACK TAR 62
REVELATION 63
CATHEDRAL 64
LONDON 65
THE BELLS OF EVENSONG 66
ALL THINGS BRIGHT 67
DAISY 68
THE LEAST I COULD DO 69
SOME STRANGE BELIEF OF MINE 70
EVE 72
THE PROBLEM 73

THE REFUGEE 74
A FOREST ONCE.. 75
TWO DOORWAYS 76
THE LIGHT THAT OUR RUIN LETS IN 78
TO GET THROUGH IT 80
IN THE UNDER OF ALL............................ 82

IV · *Songs of the Sabbath*

THE SILENCE OF THE TREES 85
THE PATH 86
BE STILL.. 88
GARDEN POEM... 89
IN THE WOODS 90
STEP AWAY 91
BRICKS.. 92
STOP 93
YOU DO NOT NEED TO SHINE.................. 94
SABBATH POEM.. 95
A SONG THRUSH MAKES THE POET
THINK OF GOD 96
UNSEIZE THE DAY.................................... 97

BLACKBERRIES 98
THE WILD ROSE 99
BUT TODAY, THE POEM 100
THE EVER-NOW 101
ON LISTENING TO GOD 102
A VISION 104

V · *The Gardener*

JUBILATE 107
PRIMROSES 108
AN AMBITION 109
LOOK, LOOK! 110
WEEDING 111
HEAVEN 112
A GARDEN IN THE ENGLISH SUMMER 113
THE BOOK 114
DIRT 115
NOT YET ENOUGH 116
AUTUMN MORNING 117
IN NOVEMBER 118
HOPE 119

WASSAIL	120
MARY	121
THRESHOLD	122
RAIN	124
SNOWDROP	125
WILDFLOWERS	126
GETHSEMANE	127
MAGNOLIA	128
THE GARDENER	129
SPRING	130

Coda · What heights

STORM IN THE EARLY HOURS	135

Acknowledgments	139
About	141

RUMOURS OF LIGHT

Prelude

IT IS TIME

IT IS TIME

Turn your gaze upon your soul, for it is time.
Look past the shadows, look between the light;
it has been waiting –

waiting for you to step back
from the endless undertakings,
to take your leave from the busyness of existence,
to release (let us say it) the obligations,

to realise that you are here.

Turn your gaze upon the world, for it is time.
Reach out to it, afraid or otherwise;
it has been waiting –

waiting for you to wake up,
to open your heart entirely to wonder, to beauty,
to the divine (that is, to the abundance
and generosity of reality).

Do not delay; let us bow to the surge of grace
that comes with each breath; let us embrace the gift
that is each singular and heaven-scented moment.

My friend, my good and worthy friend –
it is time.

Part I

BLACKBIRD

NIGHT WILL FALL ON YOU

Night will fall on you.
Of course it will.

You will find yourself
wandering the desert of your failures.
You will stand by the deathbed of your dreams,
helpless and afraid.

What hope do we have then?

Beloved, when Spirit wrapped itself
in the Rabbi's flesh, it declared
that we are to have life in all its fullness.
Yet we have forgotten that death
is part of life, that existence grows
from decay.

We have forgotten that night
is an opportunity
to anticipate
another sunrise.

GENESIS

Before the beginning there was a blank page,
an empty space onto which would be written
the most astonishing story.

Before the beginning there was an image,
a vision of generosity and power
and inspiration and compassion
and beauty and mercy and grace –
an image in whose likeness you are made.

Before the beginning
there was a singularity of possibility,
an infinitely small dot, heavy as the heart of God,
pulsating with the shining imagination
of potential, of all that could be,
of all that was and is and will be:

all of the wonder and the mud,
all of the laughter and the stars,
all of the wildflowers
and the dark matter
and the bleeding hearts,
all of the rage and the ruin
and the redemption and the dancing
the fingers entwining
and the galaxies colliding

and the birth and the death
and the smiles and the tears and the salvation.

Before the beginning
there was an intake of breath,
the divine lungs filling with fire and beauty
and the shaking multitude of souls;
there was a pause, a grin,
and then a word – begin.

There was a symphony of light
a thunderclap of creativity
the universe tripping over itself
in the becoming of its becoming
exploding evolving emerging
unfolding for the sheer thrill of it.

And moving through it all,
weaving among the miracle and the ferocity,
a gentle, powerful, playful voice,
singing over everything,
over especially and emphatically you:

It is good. It is good. It is good.

BLACKBIRD

Over the years
I've heard many sermons
telling me that I need to read
the Bible –
that this how we hear from God.

For a while I believed this,
but then I read it,
and learned that the Word is everywhere.

And so this morning
as I was half-heartedly studying
the parable of the farmer sowing seed
(the abundance of the harvest
when it falls on good soil)
I heard from outside
the first tender notes of the blackbird's song.

Letting the book fall shut
I rose from my desk
opened the door to the garden
and let the divine voice
sink in.

SUNRISE

You don't need to make your own hope –
the sky is full of it.

Wake up early one day
(I dare you)
and watch the sun rise,

watch how it encourages the Earth
to become itself, only more so,

watch how it allows all things,
even the sad beings,
to be colourful, and beautiful,

then listen, listen as it says
quietly, yet undoubtedly,
'We begin again.'

I JUST HAD THE MOST UNPRODUCTIVE MORNING

I just had the most unproductive morning.

All I did
was stare out of the window
as a playgroup of house sparrows
picked berries from the pyracantha

while a blackbird
(whose beak was dirty
from digging through the rich fat
of the soil) simply stood content
on the fence.

I just had the most unproductive morning.
Thank God.

CAMPING IN SPRING

I simply had to.
Sleep is wonderful, but the sound I heard
was so thrilling,
so pleased with something
that I had to get up
and see for myself.

It began with a single robin
leaking into my tent,
then before long
the whole place
was dripping
with the music
of a world brought to light.

I unzipped the door to the tent
– the sound of a promise
being opened –
and then saw
what all the fuss
was about.

WHEN GOD COMES TO VISIT

Do not expect thunder
or lightning.
A fanfare is unlikely.

It will not be obvious if what you expect
is the grand, the opulent.
You will not go blind.
Neither will your hair turn white.
Do not expect an old man with a beard
(do not, indeed, expect a man)
or a heavenly choir.
An earthly choir may do,
if you take the time to listen.

An example:
I had been doing the simple things –
reading a book, washing the dishes,
just ambling around,
nothing extraordinary,
when out of the window
I saw a redwing.

It was standing on the branch
of a silver birch, not moving much
except for the occasional tilt or turn of the head.
Nothing extraordinary.

. . .

It was not looking for food;
it was not singing;
it was not searching – this much was clear –
for anything. Its speckled breast
caught the light of the February evening, perhaps
the slightest touch of warmth.

I stared and I stared at it;
I felt my soul breathe out.
Nothing extraordinary.

WAKING EARLY

You may think me contrary,
but when weariness overtakes me
I do my best to wake up early.

Today, after many days
(perhaps weeks, or months, or more)
of so much life draining away
I rose at dawn.

The world does not revolve around us,
but, my God, we are part of the same revolution,
sent out by the same quiver of Christ's heart.
All of which is to say,
why wouldn't a pale morning on the first of May
know that the bones of my soul are so heavy?

Today I woke up early,
and a mist was softening the edges,
and buds had appeared overnight
on the roses, and the blackbirds
were heralding the arrival of a sun
that was an endless promise
endlessly fulfilled.

THE GEESE

Perhaps we are looking for courage
in all the wrong places –
relying too much
upon our imagined strength,
leaning too hard
upon the actions of others,
waiting too longingly for fate
to chance its arm.

Where, then, do we find it?

Look here. Spring approaches
and the geese are on the move.
I see them now, high above,
wings beating to the rhythm of life.

I do not know where they are going,
but they do. They are certain of it.

MIRACLES

It's not always the big miracles –
the thunderous, pulsating,
ground-shaking ones –
but those that are small,
delicate, unheralded:

like when the sobs finally stop,
or when the anxiety begins to fade,
or when the blackbird decides
that there is enough light
to begin praising the new day.

It's when your broken heart
eventually accepts
that it can begin to heal,
or when the delicate stem
pushes through the dirt
to discover that air and light are real.

It may just be
to open your eyes
after a night at the end of your rope,
to find that your lungs are ahead of you
and never stopped breathing in hope.

. . .

It's not the big miracles,
not the ones that shout
and shine,
it's the small miracles
that are sent to show us
the loving hand
of the divine.

STEPPING OUTSIDE AT FIRST LIGHT

Why do I not do this every time?
Watch as the dawn
spills its holy light
over the dark canvas
of the trembling night?

Why do I not do this every day?
Listen as the birds
open their throats to proclaim
that redemption is alive
as they call out its name?

Why so often do I stay inside?
Perhaps I believe
that it's better to hide
than be shown the hand of God,
and have to decide.

HOW UNEXPECTED

How easily are the legs of life
swept from beneath us;

how nonchalant the gods
who step upon our backs;

how frail seems the hope
we are told might lift us;

how unexpected, then,
when it does.

THE LATE SPRING DAWN

To listen to the chorus
of the late spring dawn
one has to wake up early;
5am will do in April –
earlier still in May.
Understandably this is why
many people never hear it.
Understandably this is why
many people believe
that heaven is far away,
or that the Earth
is a lonely place.

A NEW LIGHT ARRIVES

Buried in the night,
anxious thoughts
crowded darkly around me.

The last thing I expect is a miracle;
the last thing I anticipate
is God
riding the dawn.

But then,
like the only answer we ever need,
a new light arrives,
splashing grace-paint
on the worn-out canvas
of my heart,

and all of a sudden
hope is running along the tops of the trees
wild-eyed
and rampant.

HIDE AND SEEK

If you decide to play hide and seek
with the divine
then don't be surprised
if she loses her patience.
Don't be surprised
if she plays unfair.

Like this morning.
I had been hiding for weeks,
and so in a sacred fit of frustration
Spirit threw herself into the sky
making it every shade
of pink and blue and gold.

Naturally my heart was made bright
with wonder; naturally my soul
came out from behind its curtain.

'Ha!' I heard God say.
'Found you.'

TO BEGIN THE DAY BRIGHT

It is no easy thing,
to begin the day bright,
not when that darkening light of a screen,
unloading all the world's noisome information,
is the first thing we see.

No wonder our shoulders
and backs are sore,
carrying all of that weight.

There is relief: in the phone locked away,
unlooked for; in the simple morning
taken slow;
in the heart that gentle smiling
bows to the rising sun;
in the door pushed open
so the song of the robin pours in –
a stream that you can follow
into all that is wonderful.

It is no easy thing,
to be steadfast
in the truth of ourselves,
to not let those carrion voices
(the barking opinion, the manipulation,
the filtered picture of another life)

burrow into us,
to let instead
all that is supple and lovely in us
move over thresholds of separation
into that great belonging –
bodies brushing the welcoming grass,
finding its brother, the old oak,
its sisters, the muntjac deer,
three of whom I glimpsed this morning,
free from that rectangle of anxiety,
beckoning me brightly
into the woods.

MOON SONG

We all know the moon is beautiful,
yet every evening
we hide in our bedrooms,
eyes and curtains closed
while outside
the darkness
grows gorgeous.

But if we were told
that at dawn
we would lose its glamorous face forever
then surely we'd drop everything
and throw ourselves
beneath its silver magic.

We would take the hands
of those we love
and together we'd look up,
not having to say a word.

And in the morning
we'd hold each other tight,
we'd weep and we'd weep
but oh, what a night.

HOLD ON

One of the rose shrubs in my garden
had a tough time of winter.
It lost most of its leaves to disease,
and was further damaged by the January storms.
Not to mention the attack it had to endure
from my pruning shears.
It has been left a ragged, unlovely twist
of stem and thorn.

And yet, it is not dead.

As spring approaches, something within its cells
is saying Now.
Something within its sleepy green mind
is saying Yes.

And new leaves are beginning to grow.
And a few months from now... it is hard to describe
how lovely. How the pink
will be a shock of fresh delight each morning.
How the fragrance swimming in the warm sun
will be like a thousand dreams remembered.

Hold on, you who have been winter-wrecked.
You are not dead. Spring approaches – and beyond.

Part II

THE CUP YOU HAVE

I SEE YOU

I see you – there in the shattering you
looking for you; seeking your self
in the can't-cope of it;
the never-ending weary of it.
I see you – desperate for your soul
to be a more solid thing; to be found
amid the pantheon of the real.
I see you – wondering if God
is just the translucence of a dream.
I have been there in the lostness;
I have tangled with the shadows;
I will tell you – won't you know it? –
that something is reaching for your hand.

WHAT MANNER OF SACRED BEING

What is this stunning creature
that your skin
keeps under wraps?

What is it precisely
that your bones have grown so strong
to protect?

Those arteries of yours
that soft and relentless heart

those synapses and cells
and cloud-splitting nerves
what is it

who could it be
what manner of sacred being
is reading these words

out there in the world
alive
and eternal?

DOUBTS

You don't need to hide
from your doubts.

Let them come to you.
Let them fill you
with their peculiar magic
and show you
that the path is generous,
that it will accept more questions
than you could possibly ask.

Let your uncertainty
be the teacher you always needed –
the one who smiles
with a glint in their eye
and answers, 'Maybe.'

HOW TO BE MORE ALIVE

First, open your arms to your own humanity;
give the gorgeous mess of your entirety
a warm welcome,
remembering that all of you is loved,
free from limit or condition.

Second, drop your heart into a pool of wonder –
that sacred, healing water
found among the stillness,
among the trees and the birds
and the streams and the hills
and the opulence of an unfiltered sky.
Do not let the screens hem you in;
seek instead the heaven-wrought, the spirit-woven –
all that brightly sings of the Abundance.

Third, let your love travel beyond all bounds,
let the curtains tear before it
so that nothing is left unadored –
including the brokenness of you,
of us all.
Every soul walks with a limp,
and not one is unworthy of compassion's embrace.

And finally, remember. Remember your divine heritage.
Remember the holy sacrament poured out for you

in the form of a gentle man's blood.
Remember that the cold shackles of death
could not hold him,
could not stop him
from coming back for you.

LOVE

The ground that hatred has gained
will be retaken by love,
the losses that we've sustained
will be remembered by love,

the tears that we've cried
will be wiped away by love,
the pain and grief inside
will be healed by love,

a world that seems divided
will be remade by love,
this fight is one-sided –
the universe was built by love

and it was made to bring us together;
love is patient, kind, formidable, invincible
and it's the only thing that will last forever.
Not even death can defeat love.

So all of the sorrow and the loneliness,
all of the anger and bitterness and confusion
and brokenness will be outflanked, outdone,
outmatched and overcome by love.

DON'T SETTLE

Don't settle for a pale copy of reality –
scratching your life on tracing paper
instead of splashing your own colours
upon the expectant canvas of the world.

Don't settle for a blurred version of existence –
hyperventilating among the tangle of your busyness
instead of slowly, deeply inhaling
the limitless miracle of now.

YOUR LIFE

I need you to feel this.
I need you to know in the midst of this madness
that your life is real.

That blood charging through your veins
on a mission to make you vibrant;
those thirsty eyes soaking up
the generous light of the world;
that mind of yours, too often afraid
yet itself a God-ray, a thing of beauty –
no one is making them up.

And your soul (which if you saw,
oh the tears of joy, of gratitude, of apology)
yes, that too.

You don't need permission
to splash around in your aliveness.
The heavens may well be asking for it.

A brighter thing than this world
is calling to you, shouting at you,
desperate to let you know
that you can be kind to yourself –
that you can love wildly
your own body and spirit

exactly as they are.

It doesn't matter what has been earned
or not
for we are here –
the book has been opened
and the whole thing is moving forward
one diamond moment
at a time.

MIRROR

If you find
that you don't like
what you see in the mirror
don't worry –
it's not the real you.

You have a spirit
that existed
before you were born,
you have a smile
that was conceived
before time began,
you have a self
that can't be tainted
by what you
or anyone else
feels or thinks.

If you find
that you don't like
what you see in the mirror
don't worry –
because the real you
is deep within,
staring at you
adoringly.

WE TOO ARE SHINING BORN

I have heard a rumour,
a whisper from a distant hallelujah,
a lonely breath of light from a long-forgotten star
brushing against the remnant of our aching hearts
to tell us something beautiful,
something scarcely believable:

we too are shining born, loved extravagantly
even as our soul-lights flicker
in the blast of an unkind world.
Even in the midst of fading evidence still, so I hear,
a finer and more honest imagination than ours
declares us bright, and worthy, and good.

THE CUP YOU HAVE

Live with your heart facing outwards.
Feed your senses upon the wild-light graces
that tread the banks of the rivers;
that wander amid the hallowing of the trees.

Release your spirit to its original attitude;
the one of blessing, and curiosity, and gift.

Do not run from the darkness –
hidden in the folds of the night
are the holiest of the secrets,
waiting for you to lower your guard.

Once you have felt how heavy life is
you might quit stomping around;
once you discover how serious life is
you might stop taking yours so seriously.

We stand in awe of the angels,
but do they know what it is
to haul themselves
from the cold ground of despair?

The broken-hearted make the best dancers.

Think of it – the gravity of an entire planet

cannot prevent you from climbing a tree.

You could take little sips from the cup you have.
Most do. Most believe (and do not blame them)
that joy is in scant supply,
that they must ration themselves accordingly.

You could do that.
Or, with an open heart,
with senses and spirit uninhibited
and with the mysteries of the dark
fizzing in your bones
you could drink deep –
for you have returned to the ever-dawn of it,
for you know (there is no need to believe;
you have seen it! You have heard it bursting
from the springs of time)
the generosity,
the abundance of life.

THERE YOU ARE

Free from ambition,
from the desire to please,
free from striving and straining
and the need to succeed;

free from the rat race,
from the struggle to be first,
free from grasping and clutching
and the ego's desperate thirst;

free from vanity,
from wearing a false face,
free from image and status
and pride's fruitless chase;

free from possessions,
from diluting life with stuff,
free from other people saying
that you aren't enough;

free from your past,
from any bruise or scar,
free from guilt, free from shame –
there you are.

LET ME NOT BE GRACEFUL

Let me not be graceful;
let me not be pristine, proper,
whatever is expected of me
these days.
I want to make a scene
before heaven's wide eyes;
I want to be scandalous
in the force of my love
for this breath;
I want there to be God
beneath my fingernails –
body slick with spirit
and with sweat.

SCALPEL

The Holy Spirit
took out a scalpel
while I lay motionless
on the operating table.

I knew that it would hurt.
I knew from years of experience
that I could not get away.

The first slice
went through skin,
the second through muscle
and the third through bone.
She pushed her slender fingers
in, pinched, and pulled out
a bloody sample.

She placed it under a microscope
and studied it for a while.
There was a shake of the head,
a few mutterings
of disapproval.

Then suddenly she whipped around
and looked right at me,
and I felt the wound bubble

and hiss
from the glory;

'What do you see?'
I stammered.

'I see life, desperate
to be lived. I see
the divine image,
and gifts that only you can give.

'I see all these things,
clear
and true,
and I see the fear
that is keeping them locked
within you.'

AN ANCIENT TUNE

I have never felt more alone,
surrounded as I am
by comfort and achievement,
possessions and convenience.

Desires fulfilled, I hear the darkness
laughing at me.

Meanwhile, all that I need
(rarely what is taught or believed)
hums quietly an ancient tune,
waiting patiently
for me to hear it.

YOUR UNGODLY SOCKS

The entrance to heaven
is not a pearly gate
to be prised open
by the stale, rigid bodies
of the devout.

The way to the divine is endless
and everywhere
and you can stagger through
hand in hand
with the rejects
and the vagabonds
laughing your ungodly socks off.

TO LIVE

Do you think that your life has a purpose?
Do you believe that it should?
What is it you are meant to be doing
with the tangle of light and shadow that is you?

***

I asked the gods
(there were three on this occasion)
if it was enough just to live.

One of them began to sob.
One of them – truly –
got down on their knees and began to pray.
And the last one it seemed was struggling to contain
their laughter.

As I was leaving, this god, now in fits of giggles,
caught up with me, gesturing to the wide doors
that led outside, 'Yes! Of course yes! But my friend,
what do you think that living is?'

***

Once you have the right question
you might discover that you already have the answer.

* * *

The angels are not writing an evaluation,
they are simply gazing (a little awestruck)
into your face, waiting for your eyes
to widen in wonder,
your mouth to arise into a smile,
your cheek to be blessed with tears.

You only have to live.
Every creature except the human being
will tell you this.

* * *

If I am to do one thing it must be this:
to teach you that the Earth is a gift
to be joyfully and solemnly received,
and that you yourself have a gift
to be joyfully and solemnly given.
Life – yes, the life that you so crave –
is this simple, this gentle exchange.

* * *

I walk beneath the trees,
oak and ash and beech,

each one content (and nothing could convince me otherwise)
with both its uniqueness
and its utter reliance on all that is not itself.

In the holy earth, the tips of their roots intertwine
with the long fingers of fungus that cross the soil,
sharing sustenance and information
and who knows what else
with the greater web of life.

A prophet could not have said it better.

***

Do you think you are self-sufficient?
Do you think you are self-made?
Do you think you can do it on your own?
The air would beg to differ, as would the flesh
of the plants, and the animals.

Let us speak then – and without cynicism – of love.
Let us give thanks that we are not alone.
Let us know it deeply.

***

The sun and the rain and the soil give life.
The world offers freely its beauty and delight.

Reciprocate.

***

Tell me, friend,
have you loved today?
Have you set the fruits of the earth upon your plate
and made a proclamation of grace?
Have you let your body know that it is real,
have you moved it through the gorgeous world
of which it is a gorgeous part?

Is life enough? Are you?
When we are not bothering the gods
with our search for answers
they are dancing.

Part III

DARK MATTER

CAGE

I know it can seem
as though you are in a cage,
as though your tender mind
is being contorted into shapes
that you cannot dare name.

I know it can seem
as though nothing exists beyond it,
that the world is small and grey.

I will not tell you it is easy to escape
but know this: if you want I will stay
and make you a cup of tea.
For what happened to you
has also happened to me.

THE ELOQUENCE OF LIGHT

Sometimes we need the darkness,
sometimes we need the night,
for the cold heart of winter
is where we find
the true eloquence of light.

Sometimes we need to be broken,
sometimes we need to let go,
for pruning the branches
is often required
to allow new flowers to grow.

DARK MATTER

Do not show me your bright stars;
we cannot grow
among the shine and the glitter;

show me instead your dark matter,
lead me to the places
where those stars collapsed;

let's fall towards the blackness together,
across the event horizon
into something better.

LONELINESS

I would trade
in a heartbeat
all the light
poured upon me
for one friend
to sit with
in the dark.

THE DEATH OF GOD

It is not the philosophers
who are killing God.
It is not the atheists
or the scientists
or even
the fundamentalists.

It is the chemicals
being sprayed on the fields;
the tarmac
suffocating the earth;
the neon fog
hiding the glory of the stars;

it is the endless cages
the trees being torn down
the blank multitudes
thinking only of indoors
while holy words
fade from our minds –
like hawthorn and turtledove,
field mouse and red campion.

This is the slow
and agonising death
of God.

BLACK TAR

Lord, if I whispered a prayer
would you hear it?
Would you hear if I shouted?
They are so delicate,
and I fear mine would be drowned out
by the traffic
and the planes
and the legion voices yelling again and again
that they want more.

I fear even if there was silence
the prayer would still get scrambled
by free wi-fi
and unlimited data
and GPS signals telling us exactly where we are
on this Earth that we're tearing apart.

I fear even if it did get through
and you sent an angel to help me
she would never reach me –
she would collapse by the side of the road,
silver lungs choking on the fumes,
coughing up the acid tar
of our indifference.

REVELATION

I stumble into a chamber
that was once the Earth.
The dark is close. Closer than my sweat.

I walk upon silent bodies
that should be cold, but have been kept warm
by a long-ago lit furnace.

Nothing grows here.

At the end of the chamber
there is a broken throne.
If I squint, I can see through the smoke
what might have been a god,
head in its hands, body shaking in sobs
that no one will hear.

CATHEDRAL

I found it among the cliffs,
near the chanting bird sanctuaries
and the offering of a platinum sea.
'Danger: deep excavations.'
Warnings about explosions.
A giant rock carving that isn't art.

In this place?
In this hallowed space
of candyfloss wildflowers
and bluebells praying before the waves
and butterflies that can stop time?

By the entrance to the quarry
there was another sign,
boasting of how the blasted rocks
had been used to build cathedrals.

Men. We blow up heaven
then build a lesser imitation
somewhere else.

LONDON

I walk the streets
of this grand city
and see progress
screeching past
tearing up the trees
and the children
in its ambitious path.

THE BELLS OF EVENSONG

If I lay still for long enough
I can hear the faintest echo
of the bells of Evensong.

Deep in the long past
I walk through wide church doors
and into candlelight;
there I find a seat
next to the Holy Ghost, who is always
so quiet. She likes to listen
to the choir, who breathe out rumours
of some heaven,
whose harmonies are the best kind of sermon.

Now I walk into church
and all the lights are fluorescent
and everyone is shouting out answers
instead of listening
for a better question.

I do not see the Holy Ghost.
I wonder if she, like the bells of evensong,
is slowly fading into whatever it is
that was once a memory.

ALL THINGS BRIGHT

A raptor owns the sky
above the village in which I live.

And as I watch him circling I think:
everything about this unsafe creature,
wings and talons and beak and mind
has been shaped, evolved, created, designed
to kill, and kill well –
to snuff out in one crashing moment
a soft, warm body.

So if we are to sing
of all things bright and beautiful,
if we are to love (and we must love)
this Earth,
then we must open our voices
and our hearts
to the death bird.

DAISY

If you want your mind to shrink,
if you want reality to shrivel
until it's little more
than a wrinkled bag
then revere nothing,
dwell only in the inorganic
and mechanical,
never bow before the immensity
of even the daisy,
on whose white wings
you will find
the fingerprints of God.

THE LEAST I COULD DO

There is the dawn poem, the spring poem,
the blackbird singing after rain poem;
there is the rose poem, the kiss poem,
the soul bathing in warm light poem.

I have written all of these, and done my best,
my best being the least I could do
in a world whose most nonchalant sunrise
can leave me in raptures.

But there is also the dark poem, the cold sweat poem,
the head buried in your hands poem;
there is the grief poem, the broken poem,
the wading out into a writhing sea poem.

I have written all of these too, and done my best,
my best being the least I could do
in a world whose mountains do not care
whether you ascend their summits
or slip off
into the void.

SOME STRANGE BELIEF
OF MINE

These faded stains,
these scars that still itch,
these pale strands of midnight's hair
found among the sheets;

these fermenting proverbs,
these church bells that don't want to be rung,
these shattered limbs of hallelujah light
that once promised to hold me;

these dead canaries,
these smashed fox-cubs by the side of the road,
these elders of the wood torn down
because too many of us have never been enchanted;

these mocking pages,
these taunts of backspace backspace backspace;
these attempts to crawl into that space that exists
in the thin gap between pain and God;

and these blades of grass growing in spite of it all;
these worms renewing the soil in spite of it all;
these cells in my tired body dying and dying
and being replaced in spite of it all;

. . .

these crumbling passages of hope,
these defiant flags raised above a burning parapet;
these butterflies landing on a pinprick of morning
daring me to dream that one day it will be okay.

I write these words, these attempts to put my hand
into the bloody side of Christ,
because there are days when I want to die,
yet some strange belief of mine
makes me think that if I keep creating and creating
and those forms start touching
someone else's shattered heart
then perhaps, perhaps,
we can keep this damned thing going.

EVE

Up she rose
and straight away
she felt the eyes upon her.
She walked in the garden
and it wasn't just the snake
who put his lies upon her.
To exile they went
and without a complaint
she took the weight upon her.
Men wrote the Word
and ever since the world
has been laying its hate
upon her.

THE PROBLEM

After a while
the problem became obvious.
And so it was that Christ returned
and tried to set things right.
Many of the faithful were surprised,
but those who didn't leave
got used to it eventually.
'Rabba,' they asked,
'teach again us how to pray.'
And she said to them,
'Our Mother,
hallowed be your name…'

THE REFUGEE

It was months, perhaps years ago.
No one seems to know exactly how long.
What is recorded is this:
the bloated body of a young woman
was found in the sea;
brown skin, calloused hands
and strange scars.
A survivor from the boat
said that he had spoken to her:
'She said strange things –
that a kingdom was once at hand,
that the world had not understood.
She kept asking again and again
"Have I failed? Have I failed?"
When the storm came she rose to her feet
and it seemed she might say something else.
Then she sat down again.
When the boat capsized
she was thrown into the waves.'

After they had pulled the body out,
after the water had emptied from her lungs
they buried her in an unmarked grave.
Rumour has it that there is proof;
that if you want, you can go and see
the bones.

A FOREST ONCE

I thought I dreamt of a forest once, darkfully green,
a place where the wind could hide
and becoming lost we would find ourselves.

I thought I dreamt of fallen leaves,
of decay enriching the soil – life rising
from the sweet sting of impermanence.

Now awake, encased by undying concrete,
I think of the beginnings that will never come
because of the endings that cannot.

TWO DOORWAYS

Why are we so eager to win?
What is this victory
to which so desperately
we're trying to cling?

Live with love and eventually
inevitably
you will lose.

The sacred way is no triumph;
it is a falling off;
it is a letting go;
it is a growing awareness
that living in abundance
means to bear the unbearable.

But we are hoping. My God
we are hoping.

Open yourself to love's outpouring
and one day there will be
the piercing,
the emptiness rising,
the dark soil tipped off the shovel
and the sound as it hits what we will
but cannot face.

. . .

There are two doorways to death.
One of them is called love.

Many summers ago, I knelt
before a shrine of peonies,
inhaling an air that changed me.
The flowers are nothing now;
except in my memory;
and that of the ground.

My God, I am hoping.

To love is to climb the mountain knowing
that every step might be the one to break your spirit;
that some strange god will whisper to you
along the way;
and that all that waits at the cloud-veiled summit
is silence.

Yet still I say
to each and every one of you
do not for one moment hesitate.
Lace your boots. Shoulder your pack.
Stride up. Stride up.
There are two doorways.
Stride up.

THE LIGHT THAT OUR RUIN LETS IN

There is the falling. The breaking.
The tearing open. The pulled apart.
The head buried in the hands.
The fists pounding on the floor.
The shrieks and the sobs and the why
and the why
and the why.

This is the broken heart; the grief; the failure;
the betrayal; the disappointment; the loss;
the leaving the garden behind.

There is the waking up in the wilderness.
The long and trembling wait.
The glimpses of movement in the shadows.
The pale beginning. The unexpected expansion.
The deeper rivers discovered. The reality uncovered.
The truth rushing up. The love pouring in
and pouring in
and pouring in.

This is the dawn that the darkness brings;
the light that our ruin lets in;
the gold filling the cracks in our shattered selves.

. . .

There is the realisation. The astonishment of grace.
The heart that knows why it was made.
The response.
The renewed or newly discovered purpose.
The opening up. The reaching out.
The tentative steps forward growing bolder
and bolder
and bolder.

This is the move from I to us, from me to we;
the fierce and tender hope
that only eyes that have wept can see;
the journey that is goodness, is a terrible beauty,
is the message that is written in the blood of God.

TO GET THROUGH IT

You can't avoid the grief
or ignore the broken heart,
you can't go around the pain
if you want something new to start.

To get through it,
you have to go through it.

Healing won't come all at once,
not every tunnel has light,
before you reach the dawn
you must hold fast through the night.

To get through it,
you have to go through it.

Hope isn't interested in haste,
dreams follow a strange design,
you cannot cheat the mystery of fate
or peer through the veil of time.

To get through it,
you have to go through it.

So don't long to be somewhere else,
wishing your life away –

it's a precious ache of a journey
to be taken day by day

and to get through it,
you have to go through it.

IN THE UNDER OF ALL

And now, bitten through by fate,
you have come to the marrow of yourself.
With all that breaking apart
here lies the naked centre –
the irreducible particle
in which everything finds its mass.

And here, after being dragged through
all that darkness, after crossing
the dead waters, there in the under of all
you will find
that shining
light.

Part IV

SONGS OF THE SABBATH

THE SILENCE OF THE TREES

There is a grace
that we cannot remember,
a peace that has passed
our understanding.

For who cares to listen
to the silence of the trees?
Who ventures out into the quiet
of their own soul?

Who in this age of deafening hurry
can find that gentle answer
hidden so wisely
in the heart of an autumn leaf?

THE PATH

You can step away
from the treadmill now.
We both know how tired
you have become;
we both know how the noise
has been driving you mad.

I won't blame you for getting on
in the first place. We were all lied to.
We were all told
that it led somewhere.
Look how many increase the speed
hoping to get there faster;
see how inevitably
they fall.

I am glad to have reached you.
Come away now. Come out into the sun,
into the wind and the rain.
Here is a path.
I cannot tell you how long it is,
or the wonders, the tragedies you will find
around its sharp corners
(but, Christ alive,
if you open your heart as much as your eyes
you will find them).

. . .

I can tell you that it will end in your death –
of course! And why would we forget?

The ground is solid, but softer than you might think.
You can sit down anywhere
and admire the view.
You are encouraged to make a habit of rest.

At many points it will branch off
and you won't know which path to take.
Do not be convinced that it matters.
But take note of this:
in all places it is wider
than one set of shoulders.

BE STILL

Be still,
for that is where life removes its veil,
offering a tender grace
that will ease you away
from the cold chains of doing.

Be still, for only in shedding
your dead skin of busyness
can you find what it is to be free –
which is un-evaluated time,
which is gratitude
for the soft arms of existence,
that despite squeezing too tight now and then
will nonetheless hold you

until the time comes to let you go,
allowing you to dwell in that greater stillness –
the loving silence of the unknown.

GARDEN POEM

You cannot argue
with a garden.
There is no debate
in the chamber
of cherry-blossom.
When the camellias bloom
there is no room
for discourse.

IN THE WOODS

In the woods
it is as quiet
as God.

Beneath the canopy
I come alive
listening
to the sap
rising

thinking
only
in the language
of the roots

who move
at the speed
of heaven.

STEP AWAY

My darling, look up
from your work
for a while. Listen.
Music is falling from the stars
past the window
you keep locked shut.

Open the eyes and ears
of that gorgeous soul
and you will notice
that the whole universe
is a love song written for you.

Step away from your worries
for a while. Put your sighing arms
around my shoulders
and dance with me. Let's dance
while God's orchestra
plays us into the shining night.

Let's move our holy bodies
until the end of time,
then, afterwards,
make the soft grass our bed,
and stay there
for whatever is next.

BRICKS

The weather was beating
against the hard shell
of the house, so I decided
to open the door
and find out what it had to say.

The cold greeted me warmly
while the wind asked me
why I'd hemmed myself in
behind these dead bricks of comfort.

Not having a decent answer,
I stepped outside
into the swirling, living air
and, for what seemed the first time,
smiled.

STOP

It's amazing what can happen
when you stop
and pay attention.

Lose yourself
in a garden
staring at spring's gifts

and you might see eternity
encapsulated,
God's heart unfolding

in the folding
of a butterfly's wings,
or perhaps you will uncover

a heaven of contentment
in the way
that a blackbird sings,

but only if you
stop
and pay attention.

YOU DO NOT NEED TO SHINE

You do not need to shine.
If the feeling is too much
then neither do you need to rise.

If the floor is all you can manage right now,
if all you desire is to hide
beneath a blanket of darkness
that is fine;
you have no obligation to be at your best.

Listen to the voice within you,
the one that is silence,
the one that is rest.

SABBATH POEM

This day doesn't need
your achievement.
The earth has had enough
of performance and endeavour.

What life requires now
is the measured breaths
of the unhurried;
the close attention
of the quiet
and the still;
the gentleness that comes
from being content
with what you have.

A SONG THRUSH MAKES THE POET THINK OF GOD

After perhaps fifteen minutes or so
I gave up looking for the song thrush.
Not because I am impatient
(though there is that);
not because I didn't want
my coffee to get cold
(though there is that);
no, it is because I realised
that as long as I was searching
I was not listening,
as long as my mind was grasping
my heart was not receiving,
as long as my eyes were straining
to see the source of the music
I could not stop
to revel in the fact
that there should be music at all.

UNSEIZE THE DAY

Unseize the day;
release your grip
from the wrists of time.
Allow your plans
to drift away;
to live is to let go,
not to climb.

BLACKBERRIES

What does God want with me?

I used to believe
it was something grand –
seismic, even. It would probably,
almost certainly, involve success,
and acclaim.

How wonderfully wrong I was.

All I have to do
to satisfy heaven's desire
is go and pick blackberries
in the rain.

THE WILD ROSE

On the edge of the road
the wild rose blooms.

I pass it each morning
hurried and urgent in my car

and for a moment I am split
between the man who is going

and the creature who is there
kissing light with the rose

laughing
and blooming.

BUT TODAY, THE POEM

Lately, discord.
Life all hurry and display
and marching up a hill
in a very straight line.

But today, the poem.
It came to me
and began to harmonise,
saying why not leave
this beaten path,
let go of thoughts of up
and down?
Why not even sit for a while,
beautifully idle?

Why not, says the poem to you,
quit the rush
before you get ahead
and realise
you've left your life behind?

THE EVER-NOW

Why is it always awake and away?
Why not make only here?
Why not stay
and bless the ever-now
by our ever lingering in it
(which is impossible, which is
the utter necessity
the singular alive
so often and increasingly avoided)?
And after all this why,
where is it anyway
that you think you are going?

ON LISTENING TO GOD

It requires no leap of the imagination,
no contortion of the mind.
Forget, if you can, about belief.

Be closer to the soil
than to sanctimony.

Put away the walls and the ceilings –
you will not need them.
Be near to what is alive
but cannot diminish itself with talk.
The sky will help;
it is large enough to extinguish your questions.
The trees know what to do;
follow their lead.

Look to the dancers, to all those
who know they have a body.
If you do not walk in the garden,
how will anyone join you
in the cool of the day?

Heaven's frequency is not unfamiliar;
it is one you have always known, but perhaps lost
beneath layers of dogma
and ambition

and busyness.

Search the world for what you possess within
and you are bound to become frantic.

No, it is not a leap of the imagination,
not a contortion of the mind;
but an opening, an awareness,
a realisation, an acceptance.

A VISION

A vision comes to me:
I can feel layers of sun upon my skin,
and I am aware that the light is made from me
and I from it. The day's fullness unfolds
like so many lilies; there is no necessity,
there is no lack.

The earth and sky abound with spirit
and I have nothing to do but breathe it in –
sun-lit and unobliged.
I wander,
remind my feet why they were made,
allowing them to take me nowhere in particular.

I sit beneath trees; I lie upon the grass.
I pray with ink and with paper; letting words
like gentle, warm and quiet
reveal all of the better truths.

Then, the vision fades, like any dream,
and I hurry to my next commitment.

Part V

THE GARDENER

JUBILATE

Praise be to God,
for the sun rose this morning
without bias,
without reluctance,
without condition.

Praise be to God,
for the redbreast in the treetop
carolled the light
without worrying what the world
might think of its music.

Praise be to God,
for though it seemed it might not be so
this morning I awoke,
and my eyes saw,
and my ears heard.

PRIMROSES

I crouched over
the primroses
longing
to get closer

I lowered
my head
til the petals
touched
my skin

and then
before I knew it
my heart
was falling
in.

AN AMBITION

Recently, the Spirit decided
to give me an ambition.

It was a breathtaking vision:
one that in the end
would have even the billionaires
weeping
with envy.

I was told
quite simply
to go
and plant
a garden.

LOOK, LOOK!

A few easy moments
taken in the sun;
three small birds
blessing me
with their songs;

each with their charming
particularity; each showing
(and I'd bet my life upon it)
that they are in possession
of a soul; each repeating
(and I beg you to listen)
precisely the same
refrain:

Look, look,
it is spring, it is spring!
Look, look! Life is rising
from beneath the ground.
The green river is flowing,
the green river is flowing!
It is ready
to burst
its banks.

WEEDING

The day was full of weeds –
doubts and fears and insecurities,
so I went into the garden
after getting home from work
and dug my fork
into the redeeming earth.

HEAVEN

Are you dying to see heaven?
I tell you the truth –
you have seen it already.

The earth is thick with heaven.

Anyone who has climbed a tree
knows this.

Anyone who has stood on the forgiving shore
while the ocean breathes upon them
knows this.

Anyone who has fed a bulb to the soil
and through slow seasons watched sun and rain
give everything of themselves
just so it can grow beautiful
knows this.

You needn't fly.
You needn't reach or strive.
If heaven is what you're looking for
then all you need to do
is realise that you're alive.

A GARDEN IN THE ENGLISH SUMMER

They say nothing is perfect
but wait a minute

here I am in the English summer
and my bare feet are falling into the grass

and everything is sun-gorgeous
and the swifts are in love with the sky

and the lavender is being delighted
by a crowd of bees and butterflies

the roses show what heaven means
as heat sends their fragrance through the air

and though the world goes about its business
the garden is without a care

so let me double-check:
yes, this is perfect.

THE BOOK

One of the roses in my garden, 'Timeless Pink',
cost about the same amount
as a hardcover book.

Are you a novel, rose?
Well, you are thrilling.
Are you a self-help book?
Well, you are improving me.

Or are you (the poets turn to me)
an anthology of poetry? Each glance a hint
of a world that is quickly shut away,
but does not leave you unchanged.

Rose, you are your own acclamation,
yet even so I cannot help but write this review.
For each morning I wake up
and even in the rain
(perhaps especially in the rain)
I go out to curl up into your petals.
I escape, not out of the earth but into it,
into all that is now and here,
into all that is as real and as sharp as a thorn,
as green as a stem,
or as cold as a raindrop
on a timeless pink flower.

DIRT

Have you ever wanted to leave this flesh
and stretch for the spirit in the sky?

I understand. I too am aware
of the cold and jagged edges of this life.

But allow me save you some time.

The angels can be found not up
but all around,
and if you put your ear to the ground
you might hear God
growing in the dirt.

The pious souls can leave if they want to.
I will be happy to fall
into the soil,
become one with the earth,
broken down by worms
until I am nothing more
or less
than nourishment for the roses.

Yes, let us give ourselves,
all of ourselves,
to the roses.

NOT YET ENOUGH

I dream about roses
too much, or perhaps
(and yes, and wonderful,
and the possibilities!)
not yet enough.

AUTUMN PRAYER

Help me to love myself
in the same way that I love
the sunbeam
and the scent of fallen leaves.

Help to hold myself
in the same way I am held
by the autumn morning
stretching its golden arms
around my heart.

And help me to believe
increasingly
in this world of aching wonder,
which somehow
includes me.

IN NOVEMBER

In November, I ask God to move
(green fleece zipped up, practical boots)
through the cold and overcast scene of me.

There is work to be done: to gather
(breath visible, eyes bright, leaf sounds)
all that has fallen; to rake up the dead matter;
to pile it into a corner.
And then (satisfied in honest labour)
set flame to it –
sweet smoke rising above damp earth.

In November, I ask Spirit to make a bonfire in me;
to clear the ground for winter's rest;
to believe there may be spring.

HOPE

Hope is a golden leaf
falling to the ground.
It knows that one day
it will become the soil;
it knows that one day a seed
will settle into its dark arms;
that roots, blind
but seeking still,
will spread into the deep.

WASSAIL

Bless you apple tree,
Bless the way you grow,
Bless the patience you have
In a hasty world
To be gentle, steady and slow.

Bless you apple tree,
Bless the way you live,
Bless the kindness you have
In a needy world
For the shelter and shade you give.

Bless you apple tree,
Bless the way you care,
Bless the generosity you have
In a selfish world
For the fruit you freely share.

Bless you apple tree,
Bless everything you do,
Bless the wisdom you have
In a shallow world
To be content with being just you.

MARY

She was young,
but not too young to know.
She would have seen the soldiers
marching along the road.

She would have heard, late at night, the elders
still spinning the old tales –
slavery; liberation; exile; oppression.

She would have listened to the whispers
of a final redemption.

I wonder if she believed –
if such rumours of light could take flight
after such long and bitter centuries?

I wonder how she felt
when she was told.

THRESHOLD

At the threshold of my home
I make a huddle of one.
The grass lays low
beneath the short-lived reign of frost,
a congregation bowed in lament.

The day awakens slowly,
pressing upward
against winter's unbelief.

It is New Year's Day
and I am listening for signs of hope.
My eyes cannot see them,
not upon January's dark face,
yet they are there nonetheless.

The blackbirds say it loudest,
an affirmation of grace
proclaimed from rooftops and branches
and broken garden fences.
I let it enter
not only my mind
but the deep places
hidden beneath my shivers.

The melodies know

the work they must do
so they set to it –
mending and cleansing and,
where repair isn't possible,
simply embracing.

RAIN

I do not stay away
from the forest in the rain.
Why would I?
It brings the quiet closer;
It gives the trees a different language –
dripping
from the branches
falling slow
through the furrows
in the bark.
And all the earth is softening,
and through my feet I can feel
the gratitude of the roots,
whose thirst is being quenched,
who are meeting once again
with the sky.

SNOWDROP

Observe the man – I mean
this man, parched in the midst
of all kinds of plans,
longing for the damp ground of meaning.

Observe the snowdrop – I mean
this snowdrop, risen quite suddenly
on a bare lawn, a bead of night rain
clinging to its bowed head.

See how small it is,
how utterly without
what you might call strength
or ambition. See how it makes
even winter smile.

Little wet flower,
so unhuman,
so entirely alive.

WILDFLOWERS

I sow wildflowers in the spring:
self heal and musk mallow,
cuckoo flower and foxglove,
field poppy and yarrow.
Many will not bloom until next year.
All of their heaven scents
and singing colour
and bee-thrilling nectar
will linger in the long dark, waiting
for that bright moment.

GETHSEMANE

Of course
she thought
he was the gardener,

because who else
would have
such green fingers,

who else
would have so much dirt
beneath their nails,

who else is so often found
kneeling before the flowers
than God?

MAGNOLIA

You could look to the world,
with its nail-biting, its in-fighting,
its despair and doom-and-glooming.
Or you could look to the magnolia,
whose hundred soft hearts are blooming.

THE GARDENER

So you walk through heaven's gates
(which of course are not gates,
are nothing that can be narrow,
nothing that can be closed)
and you are surprised to find yourself
not in a throne room,
but in a garden.

There are sweet peas and sunflowers,
there are bees among the lavender,
there are roses. There are thorns
on the stems of the roses.

The soil is dark,
and not unfamiliar.

Looking for the one in charge
you notice the gardener.
They are pottering about;
they are idling around;
there is dirt beneath their nails.

You notice the sort of smile that suggests
they are about to reveal
the most wonderful secret.

SPRING

All that is good is growing.
Yesterday and so many yesterdays
it seemed dead. But now
the deep God stirs in her earth,
and seed and root remember sky
and brightening make their move
towards it. Life rubs its eyes, spring
no longer a dream to sustain
through the colding days
but a reality born from sunlight
and bluebells and the sure refrain
of the chiffchaff.
All that is good is growing;
the darker season has had its time
and will do so again, a knowledge
to make these thrill bloomings
all the sweeter. The return of the swallows
is only marked because they left,
and will leave. But today in the fields
the lambs are becoming sure of their feet,
and green is dancing once more in the trees,
and in the gardens there is a tenderness
showing itself in the eyes of the flowers.
I see that I am not dead,
nor is the hope that I was once born into.
I see the meaning in our burials –

that despairing we might rise for air
and unexpectedly find it, and explore it
with lungs made new by thankfulness.
Even though the last stands of cold
may cling to us, along with the clenching memory
of winters past – all those dyings of our hearts –
even so, today and so many todays:
all that is good is growing.

Coda

WHAT HEIGHTS

STORM IN THE EARLY HOURS

The wind is a pack of wolves – unruly, free, running along the streets and through the trees. Inside we are safe, warm, the only animals in here being myself and my four-month-old daughter – a soft little bundle in her Moses basket (and what heights you descended from, face shining with the glory of God.)

I wonder if you notice the primal noises that are throwing themselves against the old bricks of our cottage. You seem happy enough, and why wouldn't you be? You are alive, and you are aware of little else.

We too have this gift, dear reader, if we would but remember it.

I read you a selection of poetry. The words I pour onto you may just be sounds for you but I imagine them being soaked up by your delicate bones. Then as you get older and as you grow, they will seep out, and without knowing you will know that the earth is a temple, waiting for you to write your story upon its gold-green walls.

You look at me and smile. I pity people who do not believe in miracles, as if they are unaware of what the wet flesh of their heart has been doing all this time.

I have so many hopes for you I can scarcely bear it. I hope the world doesn't get to you with its shackles of money and possessions and scrambling for position. Listen to the unfettered storm, nothing but itself, thrillingly itself, and my God is it strong.

You are stronger, and your whole life will be an unfolding of this truth.

I wonder whether you will be a musician, a dancer, a doctor or a gardener – how precisely you will decide to ring the bell of love. Whichever path you choose I pray it's not one that I make for you; though don't misunderstand me – I will be there, I will give you everything I have, I will lay down everything I am – but it's your path, not the one I nor society tries to lead you on.

Look instead to the fresh morning light, to your own shining spirit, and to the howling of the wolves.

ACKNOWLEDGEMENTS

Wifey – for giving me a love that empowers me to be me.

My parents – for your unending support.

Katie Tang – for your generosity and for creating such a beautiful cover.

Emily Wilson and Rachael Adams – for being my early readers, nit-pickers and cheerleaders.

My Tearfund fam – I don't know where I'd be without you.

And to all my friends and family – you are what life is made of.

ABOUT

Gideon is a poet and environmentalist who lives in Berkshire, England. He's at his happiest when walking up a mountain, drinking coffee in his garden, or climbing trees with his daughter. He has an MA in Creative Writing and is a Senior Copywriter at a global humanitarian agency.

Printed in Great Britain
by Amazon